DISCARD

W9-COO-620

A partnership between American Library Association
and FINRA Investor Education Foundation

FINRA is proud to support the American Library Association

What Is a Bank?

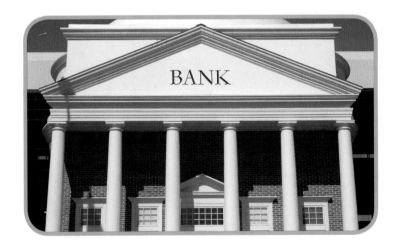

By Dana Meachen Rau

Reading consultant: Susan Nations, M.Ed., author/literacy coach/consultant

Gareth Stevens
Publishing

Please visit our Web site www.garethstevens.com. For a free color catalog of all our high-quality books, call toll free 1-800-542-2595 or fax 1-877-542-2596.

Library of Congress Cataloging-in-Publication Data

Rau, Dana Meachen, 1971–
    What is a bank? / by Dana Meachen Rau.
      p. cm. — (Money and banks)
    Includes bibliographical references and index.
    ISBN: 978-1-4339-3393-6 (pbk.)
    ISBN: 978-1-4339-3394-3 (6-pack)
    ISBN: 978-1-4339-3392-9 (library binding)
————1. Banks and banking—Juvenile literature. I. Title. II. Series.
  HG1609.R38   2005
  332.1—dc22   2005042209

New edition published 2010 by
Gareth Stevens Publishing
111 East 14th Street, Suite 349
New York, NY 10003

New text and images this edition copyright © 2010 Gareth Stevens Publishing

Original edition published 2006 by Weekly Reader® Books
An imprint of Gareth Stevens Publishing
Original edition text and images copyright © 2006 Gareth Stevens Publishing

Art direction: Haley Harasymiw, Tammy West
Page layout: Michael Flynn, Dave Kowalski
Editorial direction: Kerri O'Donnell, Barbara Kiely Miller

Photo credits: Cover, pp. 1, 4, 11, 18 back cover © Shutterstock.com; pp. 5, 6, 7, 9, 10, 13, 15, 16, 17, 18 by Gregg Andersen; p. 8 by Diane Laska-Swanke, p. 19 © Ryan McVay/Photodisc/Getty Images.

All rights reserved. No part of this book may be reproduced in any form without permission in writing from the publisher, except by a reviewer.

Printed in the United States of America

CPSIA compliance information: Batch #WW10GS: For further information contact Gareth Stevens, New York, New York at 1-800-542-2595.

Table of Contents

In the Bank. 4

Deposits and Withdrawals 7

What Is a Loan? 12

Keep It Safe 16

Math Connection:
    Keeping a Bankbook. 20

Glossary 22

For More Information 23

Index. 24

Boldface words appear in the glossary.

Have you ever lost money that you put in your pocket? It is important to keep your money somewhere safe. Where do you keep your money? You might have a small bank in your room. Some banks are shaped like animals, such as a piggy bank. Some banks have places for each kind of coin.

Many children save their money at home in small banks.

Most towns and cities have one or more banks.

One type of bank would not fit in your room. A building that holds money is also called a bank. It is like a giant piggy bank!

You may save so much money that the bank in your room is full. Then you and a parent can open a **savings account** at a bank in your town or city. The people at the bank make sure that your money is safe.

Everybody in your family can keep their money in the bank.

Deposits and Withdrawals

A **teller** will help you open a savings account. The teller is the person behind the counter at the bank. Your account will have your name on it. It will also have your parent's name on it. Now you can put money into your savings account.

A teller can answer all of your questions about saving your money at the bank.

The money you put into your savings account is called a **deposit**. You can use a **bankbook** to keep track of the money in your account. When you put money into your account, you or the teller will add the amount to your bankbook.

A bankbook is small and easy to carry.

Money you take out of your savings account is called a **withdrawal**. Your parent is the only person who can take money out of your account. The teller gives you and your parent the money you want. Then you or the teller subtracts the amount from your bankbook.

Your parent must help you take money out of your bank account when you need it.

9

People do not always need to go to a bank teller to make a withdrawal. Sometimes they do not have time to go to the bank. They can use ATMs to get money quickly. "ATM" means "Automatic Teller Machine." Sometimes people must pay extra money to use ATMs. This extra money is taken out of their account.

ATMs are a fast and easy way to get money. You might see ATMs in the grocery store, at the mall, or even at an amusement park.

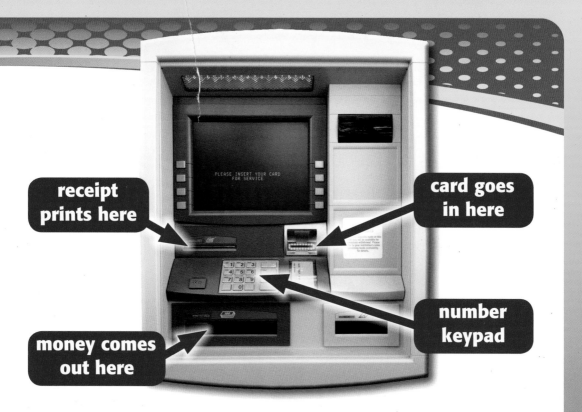

receipt prints here

card goes in here

money comes out here

number keypad

PLEASE INSERT YOUR CARD FOR SERVICE

Some ATMs, like this one, have special card slots. A person puts their card into the slot. The ATM "reads" the card's information very quickly.

Usually, a person puts an ATM card into a slot on the machine. Then he or she types in a special number code and the amount of money to take out, or withdraw. The money, a **receipt**, and the ATM card then come out of the machine.

What Is a Loan?

The bank does not keep all the money you put into your account. It uses your money to help other people until you want it. The bank puts a little extra money in your account every month to thank you for letting them use your savings. This extra money is called **interest**.

| | | | | | | SAVINGS REGISTER | | | | | |

DATE	DESCRIPTION OF TRANSACTION		WITHDRAWAL		DEPOSITS & INTEREST		BAL. BR'T F'R'D	✓			
							AMOUNT OF TRANSACTION				
							BALANCE				
							AMOUNT OF TRANSACTION				
							BALANCE				
							AMOUNT OF TRANSACTION				
							BALANCE				
							AMOUNT OF TRANSACTION				
							BALANCE				
							AMOUNT OF TRANSACTION				
							BALANCE				

A bankbook has places to write down the interest the bank pays you.

Sometimes adults want to buy something that costs more money than they have in the bank. The bank will **lend** them the money they need. This money is called a loan.

Adults must sign papers before a bank will give them a loan. This shows that they promise to pay the money back.

When you borrow a book from the library, you have to bring it back by a certain time. A bank works the same way. When a bank lends money to customers, the customers must pay the money back by a certain time. The customers must also pay the bank interest for letting them borrow the money.

The interest on a loan can be a big part of the loan payment.

Account Statement

CUSTOMER INFORMATION

Name: RUBY JOHNSON

Account Number: 1234567890
Home Phone #: (123)456-7890

PROPERTY ADDRESS

1234 PLEASANT ST.
MY CITY   USA 12345

STATE MORTGAGE

Account Activity Since Last Statement

Description	Due Date	Tran. Date	Tran. Total	Principal	Interest	Late Charge	Other
Payment	01/10/10	01/03/10	$809.55	$133.49	$676.06		
Payment	02/10/10	02/01/10	$809.55	$134.36	$675.20		
Payment	03/10/10	03/03/10	$809.55	$135.22	$674.33		

Your Payment Will Automatically Be Drafted

Mortgage Payment Coupon

Account Number	Due Date	Mortgage Payment	Amount to Be Drafted
	04/01/10	$809.55	$809.55

Check below if you need   Please assist ABCD Mortgage

Adults often borrow money to buy a house. They usually have many years to pay the money back. Other types of loans need to be paid back more quickly. Adults must pay back a loan for a car in only about four or five years. The sooner they pay back the money, the less interest the bank makes them pay.

Banks help families by giving them loans to buy their own homes.

The bank keeps some money in a **vault**. A vault is a room with a thick, locked door. Only people working at the bank can get into the vault.

The door to a bank vault is made of thick metal.

Some banks also have safe deposit boxes. Safe deposit boxes look like a wall of locked drawers in different sizes. They are like small vaults. People use them to keep things like money, jewelry, and important papers safe. Each safe deposit box has two keyholes. The customer keeps one key. The bank keeps the other key. Both keys are needed to open a safe deposit box.

People can put things in safe deposit boxes that they do not want to lose. Then they can get those things when they need them.

As you've learned, banks take the money you deposit and try to make more money with it. They might lend it to customers and charge interest on the loan. They might **invest** it. This usually works very well. The bank remains successful.

A bank employee is always willing to answer questions people have about bank accounts and bank loans.

However, if a bank makes bad decisions, it could lose a lot of money. Some banks have failed because of this. You may have heard about this on the news. Don't worry, though. The United States government protects a good portion of most people's money. The money in your savings account is safe!

Is there a game you want to buy? Do you want to buy a birthday present for a friend? You can ask your parent to take you to the bank and take money out of your account. The money you put into your bank account will be there when you need it.

Math Connection: Keeping a Bankbook

Learn how to keep track of your savings account in a bankbook. Make a copy of the bankbook on pages 20 and 21 on a separate piece of paper. Then add and subtract the numbers to find out what the total in this bank account, or its balance, would be at the end of one year.

Date	Description of Transaction
January 10	Start account
February 5	Buy a new toy
June 30	Interest from the bank
July 21	Money from chores
September 30	Buy school supplies
December 16	Gift from Grandma
December 31	Interest from the bank

	Withdrawal	Deposit	Balance
		$25.00	$25.00
	$1.00		
		$0.50	
		$5.00	
	$2.00		
		$3.00	
		$0.60	

The correct answer is on page 23.

Glossary

bankbook: a small book that shows the money put into and taken out of a bank account

deposit: an amount of money added to a bank account

interest: money that is paid or charged for the use of borrowed money

invest: to use money to buy something that will produce a profit or an income

lend: to give someone money that must be repaid

receipt: a written slip of paper that shows how much money was put into or taken out of a bank account

savings account: an account at a bank on which interest is paid

teller: the person who works behind the counter at a bank

vault: a locked room in a bank where money and valuables are kept

withdrawal: an amount of money taken out of a bank account

For More Information

Books

Armentrout, David, and Patricia Armentrout. *The Bank*. Vero Beach, FL: Rourke, 2008.

Hall, Marianne. *Banks*. New York: Heinemann, 2007.

Houghton, Gillian. *How Banks Work*. New York: Rosen Publishing Group, Inc., 2009.

Web Sites

The Mint: How Banks Work
www.themint.org/kids/how-banks-work.html
Information about saving money at a bank

Kids Bank.com
www.kidsbank.com
Information about saving money and how a bank works

Publisher's note to educators and parents: Our editors have carefully reviewed these Web sites to ensure that they are suitable for students. Many Web sites change frequently, however, and we cannot guarantee that a site's future contents will continue to meet our high standards of quality and educational value. Be advised that students should be closely supervised whenever they access the Internet.

Math Connection Answer: $31.10

Index

ATMs 10, 11

bankbooks 8, 9, 12

customers 14, 17, 18

deposits 8, 18

interest 12, 14, 15, 18

loans 13, 14, 15, 18

safe deposit boxes 17

saving money 4, 6, 7

savings accounts 6, 7, 8, 9, 12, 19

tellers 7, 8, 9, 10

vaults 16, 17

withdrawals 9, 10, 11

About the Author

Dana Meachen Rau is an author, editor, and illustrator. She has written more than one hundred books for children, including nonfiction, early readers, and historical fiction. She lives with her family in Burlington, Connecticut.

332.1 R 2010   HKENX
Rau, Dana Meachen,
What is a bank? /

KENDALL   DISCARD
08/10